GRANNY TORRELLI MAKES SOUP

by
Sharon Creech

Teacher Guide

Written by
Sharan Farmer

Note

The 2005 Harper Trophy paperback edition of the book, © 2003 by Sharon Creech, was used to prepare this guide. The page references may differ in other editions. Novel ISBN: 0-06-440960-0

Please note: Please assess the appropriateness of this book for the age level and maturity of your students prior to reading and discussing it with them.

ISBN 978-1-60539-020-8

To order, contact your local school supply store, or—

Novel Units, Inc.
P.O. Box 97
Bulverde, TX 78163-0097

Web site: www.novelunits.com

Table of Contents

Skills and Strategies

Thinking
Brainstorming, identifying attributes, compare/contrast, research, analyzing details, drawing conclusions, problem solving

Comprehension
Predicting, sequencing, main idea, inference, summarizing

Writing
Dialogue, recipe, list, journal, letter, chart, essay, mnemonic device, quiz, riddle, haiku, acrostic

Listening/Speaking
Discussion, role-play, reading Braille, foreign language, audio diary

Vocabulary
Parts of speech, definition, root words, usage, context clues, word origin, Italian vocabulary

Literary Elements
Point of view, foreshadowing, flashback, characterization, imagery, plot development, dialogue, figurative language, metaphor, simile, author's style, setting, theme, conflict, irony, sensory details, parallel story

Across the Curriculum
Art—drawing, poster, comic strip, collage; Language—Italian, Braille; Cooking—soup, pasta; Math—fractions; Social Studies—guide dogs, visual impairment, bullies; Drama—play

Genre: fiction

Setting: present-day; Rosie's family kitchen

Point of View: first person

Themes: love; life; friendship; one's place in the "bigger picture"

Conflict: person vs. person; person vs. self

Tone: serious, but occasionally humorous

Date of First Publication: 2003

Summary

Rosie and Bailey have been best friends for as long as Rosie can remember. Even though Bailey is visually impaired, it has never affected their friendship…until now. Rosie secretly learns to read Braille and is so excited to surprise Bailey with her newly acquired skill. She is shocked and hurt when he becomes angry after she reads from one of his books. Then Granny Torrelli comes for a visit. As Granny and Rosie make *zuppa* (soup), Granny helps Rosie understand that Bailey needs to be able to do some things that Rosie cannot do, such as read Braille. Rosie and Bailey apologize to each other and realize that nothing should stand in the way of their friendship.

However, a new problem soon arises. Janine, a new girl in the neighborhood, brings out feelings Rosie does not realize she has. Rosie is jealous of Janine's friendship with Bailey, especially after he offers to teach Janine to read Braille. Again, it's Granny Torrelli to the rescue! This time, as both Rosie and Bailey help Granny make pasta and sauce, she helps them realize the true meaning of life. She shows them that life is not centered around them. The author weaves humor and wisdom into the story through Granny Torrelli, as she not only cooks up soup and pasta in Rosie's family kitchen but also a few life lessons as well. Granny helps Bailey and Rosie understand these lessons by telling parallel stories of her lost childhood friendship with a boy named Pardo. By the end of the novel, Rosie realizes her world is bigger than she thought as all her family and new friends enjoy the pasta party.

About the Author

Sharon Creech was born in South Euclid, Ohio, and enjoyed being part of a large family. Although she aspired to be many things when she was young, she found her calling as a high school English and writing teacher. It was during this time of teaching the elements of plot, theme, and characterization that she learned the art of storytelling. Creech spent 18 years as a teacher in England and Switzerland and published two adult fiction books in England, *The Recital* and *Nickel Malley*. Her next novel, *Absolutely Normal Chaos*, which was based on her experiences growing up in a large family, began her writing career for young people. Her first novel to be published in America, *Walk Two Moons*, won the 1995 Newbery Medal and was based on a family trip to Idaho. As a child, Creech and her family enjoyed trips to her cousins' farm in Quincy, Kentucky. These experiences found their way into future novels as Bybank, Kentucky, in *Walk Two Moons, Chasing Redbird, Bloomability,* and *The Wanderer*, a Newbery Honor book. Other novels by Creech include *Pleasing the Ghost, Love That Dog, The Castle Corona, Heartbeat,* and

Replay. She has also written three picture books, *Fishing in the Air, Who's That Baby?*, and *A Fine, Fine School*, inspired by her husband's experiences as headmaster of a school in England. She was the first American to be awarded the Carnegie Medal, for *Ruby Holler*. Creech and her husband now live in New Jersey and have two grown children. *Granny Torrelli Makes Soup* was inspired by her anticipation of becoming a grandmother.

Characters

Rosie: 12-year-old girl; Bailey's best friend; loves to help her granny cook

Bailey: 12-year-old visually-impaired boy; Rosie's best friend; very independent

Granny Torrelli: Rosie's Italian grandmother; very observant and wise

Carmelita: Bailey's mother

Janine: new girl in the neighborhood; very friendly; inspires jealousy in Rosie

Pardo: Granny's childhood friend in Italy

Violetta: young Italian girl; was Granny's rival for Pardo's attention

Marco: young man who developed an interest in Granny; inspired jealousy in Pardo

The Jeffersons: a family that recently moved to the neighborhood

Lucille: the Jeffersons' daughter

Johnny and Jack: the Jeffersons' sons

Initiating Activities

Use one or more of the following to introduce the novel.

1. Prediction: Have students skim the novel and note the format of the book, the different font types used, the artwork, and the chapter titles. Discuss what each might mean and predict what the book will be about.

2. Prediction: Have students begin the Prediction Chart on page 18 of this guide. This activity will continue as students read the novel.

3. Creative Writing: Have students create a recipe book and use the correct format for writing recipes to add several of their families' favorites. Include Granny's recipes for soup and pasta.

4. Journal: Have students begin a "life lessons journal" and record some of the lessons they have learned about life, love, and friendship from their own families and friends. Include the words of wisdom Granny offers Rosie and Bailey. As the novel study continues, encourage students to share one or more journal entries with the class.

5. Critical Thinking: Have students brainstorm the qualities they would like a friend to have. Encourage students to compare their lists to their existing friendships and examine whether these qualities are present.

Vocabulary Activities

1. Dictionary Drills: Have students conduct dictionary drills by having one student call out a vocabulary word and having the first person that finds the word read its part of speech and definition(s).

2. Charades: Have students play vocabulary charades. Students act out selected words from the vocabulary lists while other students guess the words.

3. Mnemonic Devices: Mnemonic devices include short riddles, rhymes, poems, pictures, designs, or acronyms. Have students work in pairs to develop mnemonic devices for vocabulary words to help them remember the definitions. Assign different words to each pair, and have students share the devices they create.

4. Comprehension: Have students create quizzes for vocabulary words and trade with a partner.

5. Root Words: Have students make a T-chart using vocabulary words and their roots.

6. Crossword Puzzle: Have students create a vocabulary word crossword puzzle (see page 19 of this guide) to trade with classmates.

7. Creative Writing: Have students compose riddles about a vocabulary word, giving clues such as definition, part of speech, word origin, word relationships, etc. Then give the riddles to other students to solve.

8. Comprehension: Have students create a memory card game using the vocabulary words and their definitions.

Part I. Soup
That Bailey–Just Like Bailey

Rosie is very angry with her best friend and next-door neighbor, Bailey. While making soup in the family kitchen, Rosie's grandmother, Granny Torrelli, tries to get Rosie to discuss what has upset her so much. Rosie reflects on some of her and Bailey's earlier times together.

Vocabulary
compliment
spiteful
rooting
snatches
fling
snares
swirling
inseparable
rummaging

Discussion Questions

1. "My granny Torrelli says when you are angry with someone… think of the good things about them…" (p. 5). Is this good advice? Why or why not? *(Answers will vary. Thinking of good things about a person reminds someone of why s/he likes the other person in the first place, thus allowing her/his anger to lessen.)*

2. Foreshadowing is a literary technique that hints at a future event without actually mentioning it. The author uses this technique to hint at a problem that Bailey has. What do you think the problem might be? What are some hints that suggest your answer? *(Bailey has a problem with his sight; "[Bailey's] hands waving out in front of him, sweeping the air" [p. 8]; Rosie's mother shows her that Bailey's sight is like looking through a tissue, and Bailey goes to a different school than Rosie.)*

3. Rosie says that Bailey is "better than a brother because I chose him and he chose me" (p. 8). Why do you think she believes this? Do you agree with Rosie's assessment of friendship being better than family because of the choice involved? *(Answers will vary.)*

4. Rosie and Granny Torrelli discuss Rosie's problem while making soup. Why do you think this is easier for Rosie than sitting down and discussing her problem face to face? *(Answers will vary but may include that it is easier to talk about personal issues casually while busy with another task.)*

5. Why do you think Granny Torrelli chooses this opportunity to tell Rosie about Pardo? *(Granny was good friends with Pardo when she was a young girl and, like Rosie, had a problem with their friendship. Granny is trying to put Rosie at ease and relate to her, regardless of their age difference.)*

6. Flashback is a literary technique used to tell events that have already happened and that may be influencing present events. The chapter entitled "Bambini" is told entirely in flashback. Why is this chapter important to the story? *(Rosie tells of how she first experienced the problem Bailey has with his sight when she put the tissue over her eyes. As with the use of foreshadowing, this use of flashback gives readers an idea of what might be wrong with Bailey.)*

7. Rosie is very upset that Bailey cannot come with her on the first day of school. What do you think Rosie's mom may say to comfort Rosie while they sit on the swings in the park? *(Answers will vary.)*

8. **Prediction:** Why is Rosie so angry with Bailey?

Supplementary Activities

1. Literary Devices/Art: Imagery is a literary technique where the writer "paints" pictures with words. Choose a vivid use of imagery from this section of the novel and draw it as a picture. Example: "She frowns, a big clown frown, and pretends to sob" (p. 12).

2. Foreign Language: Begin a list of Italian words used in the novel. Use an English-Italian dictionary or the Internet to find the meaning of each word, as well as its pronunciation. Add to your list as you read the novel.

3. Journal: Add to your life lessons journal (see Initiating Activity #4 on page 4 of this guide) after reading this section.

4. Cooking: Choose a favorite soup recipe. Ask an adult to help you prepare and bring the soup to class.

Soup
Put Your Feet Up–Tangled Head

Rosie thinks a lot about the past—Bailey learning Braille, the plays they performed together, and her attempt at training a guide dog for Bailey. Granny Torrelli tells the story of her troublesome experience with Pardo's dog, Nero.

Vocabulary
distracts
mangy
fetch
slosh
straggled
prickled
loping
delicatessen
lured
ditto
slurps

Discussion Questions

1. Granny Torrelli distracts Rosie with a simple question before asking Rosie what she really wants to know. Rosie says this could be a useful skill. Do you agree? Why or why not? *(Answers will vary.)*

2. Why does Rosie lie after ripping Bailey's Braille book? *(She is jealous of Bailey's ability to read Braille. She is upset that there is something so significant separating her from her friend.)*

3. Irony is a literary term used to describe a situation that is inconsistent with what one would expect. How is Rosie's jealousy of Bailey's ability to read Braille an example of irony? *(It is more common for a person with a disability to be jealous of someone without the disability. Although Bailey cannot see well and Rosie can, she is still jealous that he can read Braille and she cannot.)*

4. Why does Bailey think it is stupid for Rosie to play the part of a blind woman? *(Answers will vary but may include that Rosie has no idea what it's like to be blind and Bailey finds it a bit offensive for her to try.)*

5. Although monologue (dialogue written for one person) is a popular form of entertainment, why do you think Rosie does not believe her monologue makes a very good play? *(Answers will vary but may include that she doesn't like to play without Bailey.)*

6. Why does Granny Torrelli punch Pardo when she returns home and sees Nero beside him? *(Answers will vary. Suggestions: She is angry that the dog returns to Pardo after she tries to win its affections and does not succeed. She may also be frustrated that she went through such an ordeal when the dog was safe at home the entire time.)*

7. Why does Rosie think Bailey should tell her everything? *(Answers will vary.)*

8. Why does Granny Torrelli describe heaven as a pasta party? *(Answers will vary but may include that she is from Italy where pasta is associated with a good meal and a good time.)*

9. When Rosie inquires further about Pardo, Granny Torrelli tells her that she "[doesn't] want to know about it" (p. 48). What are some reasons Granny may have said this? *(Answers will vary but may include that something bad eventually happened to Pardo.)*

10. Both Rosie and Granny Torrelli wish that they had each other's minds. Why do you suppose they feel this way? *(Answers will vary but may include that Rosie wishes for all the years of Granny's wisdom and experience, while Granny wishes for Rosie's youth and innocence.)*

Supplementary Activities

1. Language: Check out a Braille book from the school or public library. Using a Braille chart, read a paragraph from the book.

2. Drama: With a partner, perform the play that Rosie and Bailey make up in the chapter titled "Plays."

3. Writing: Working in pairs, write another short play that Rosie and Bailey might perform. Be sure to write your play in the correct format, using stage directions and alternating characters. Perform your play for the class.

4. Critical Thinking: Begin the Effects of Reading chart on page 20 of this guide.

5. Research: Using print and Internet resources, research the requirements for owning a guide dog.

Soup
Lost–*Tutto*

Rosie reminisces about the time Bailey got lost and found his way home and the time he rescued her from a pair of bullies. Rosie finally tells Granny Torrelli why she is angry with Bailey—she worked very hard to learn Braille to surprise Bailey, but he was unexpectedly angry and cruel when she revealed her new ability. Granny is reminded of leaving Pardo behind in Italy and how angry he was with her. Pardo died in a tragic accident before Granny could apologize, and she has regretted it every day since. Rosie learns a valuable lesson, and Rosie and Bailey apologize to each other.

Vocabulary
roaming
ghastly
whacking
parsley
flopped
smug
wail
nuisance
dazzling
fare
chattering

Discussion Questions

1. Why is Bailey never supposed to go anywhere alone? *(Bailey's mother fears that Bailey's eyesight would prevent him from finding his way home.)*

2. Bailey says that he simply "went for a short walk that got very long" (p. 53). Do you believe he was really lost? *(Answers will vary.)*

3. Rosie and Bailey are close friends, but they seem to disagree a lot. Is this typical in friendships? Explain your answer. *(Answers will vary.)*

4. Why is Bailey so angry with Rosie when he discovers she can read Braille? *(Answers will vary. Suggestions: Reading Braille is something Bailey can do that most people cannot. It is important to Bailey that he be able to do something that others consider special and challenging.)*

5. Why does Granny Torrelli cry when she hears Rosie's story? *(It reminds her of when she left Pardo. They were angry with each other when they parted, and neither of them ever apologized.)*

6. How might Granny Torrelli's life have been different had she written an apology letter to Pardo? *(Answers will vary.)*

7. What is the significance of the manner in which Bailey apologizes? *(By giving Rosie an apology written in Braille, he is showing her that he accepts the fact that she can read Braille.)*

8. Part I of the book closes with "All is well" (p. 74), however, the story continues. Predict what the rest of the book will be about. *(Answers will vary.)*

Supplementary Activities

1. Compare/Contrast: Using the Venn diagram on page 21 of this guide, list the similarities and differences between Granny Torrelli "losing" Nero and Rosie thinking Bailey is lost.

2. Social Studies: As a class, brainstorm about how to deal with bullies. Using some of the best ideas, act them out in class.

3. Critical Thinking: Continue adding to your Effects of Reading chart.

4. Writing: Think of a time when you caused a friend to feel angry, sad, or disappointed. Write an apology letter and deliver it to your friend.

Part II. Pasta
She's Back–Violetta

Granny Torrelli returns to Rosie's house one week later, and they invite Bailey over to make pasta. Granny learns that a new girl, Janine, has moved in nearby and is very friendly to both Rosie and Bailey. Rosie, however, does not enjoy Janine's affection and becomes jealous when Bailey offers to teach Janine how to read Braille. Granny tells a story about Violetta, a new girl that moved into her neighborhood in Italy, and exhibits some jealousy of her own.

Vocabulary
pastry
plucking
sifts
whisking
puckers
flattered
suspended
tilted
mangling
swooned
throttle

Discussion Questions

1. Why is Rosie upset that something else is "squeezing in between" her and Bailey? What might this "something" be? *(Answers will vary.)*

2. Granny Torrelli seems to be a very experienced cook. We know this by the fact that she never uses a recipe, she is able to prepare a meal using only the ingredients she finds in the pantry, and she never measures anything. Do you think this is a realistic representation? Have you ever known anyone who could cook well without a recipe? *(Answers will vary but may include that this is a realistic representation because some people are often able to prepare meals based on memory and experience.)*

3. Why does Granny Torrelli ask Bailey to crack the eggs into the bowl instead of Rosie? *(She wants to make Bailey feel important and useful and prove that Bailey does not need as much help as Rosie thinks he does.)*

4. Rosie calls herself an "ice girl, ice queen" (p. 84). Why? *(Whenever Rosie thinks of the new girl, Janine, her heart becomes instantly cold. Rosie is suspicious of Janine because she thinks Janine is too friendly.)*

5. How does Rosie feel during her first meeting with Janine? Do you think Rosie is too judgmental? Explain your response. *(Rosie thinks Janine is strange for wanting to be her best friend without knowing her well. Rosie is suspicious of Janine's intentions while at the same time feeling good that Janine seems to like her so much. Answers will vary.)*

6. Rosie often refers to herself in the third person, using words such as "tiger," "ice girl," and "ice queen" to describe herself. What purpose do Rosie's references to her various "selves" serve? *(Answers will vary.)*

7. Why is Rosie so angry while Bailey is describing Janine to Granny Torrelli? Do you think Bailey is aware of Rosie's feelings? *(Rosie discovers that Bailey likes Janine and thinks she is nice, funny, and curious. Rosie is extremely jealous. Answers will vary.)*

8. Why is Rosie jealous when she discovers that Bailey has agreed to teach Janine to read Braille? Do you think she should feel this way? *(Bailey never offered to teach Rosie to read Braille. In fact, he was extremely angry and hurt when he found out she had learned to read Braille. Answers will vary.)*

9. Why do you think Bailey is not angry that Janine wants to learn Braille? *(Answers will vary.)*

10. Why does Rosie "hear a little ice queen" in Granny Torrelli's voice when Granny speaks of Violetta (p. 95)? *(Answers will vary but may include that Granny was jealous of Violetta's paying so much attention to Pardo.)*

Supplementary Activities

1. Literary Elements: Using the Metaphors and Similes chart on page 22 of this guide, list examples of metaphors and similes from the novel.

2. Research: Research methods for preparing pasta. What are some similarities to the methods Granny Torrelli uses in the novel? What are some differences? Is pasta typically made by mixing the dough with your hands? Create a how-to sheet for preparing pasta.

3. Cooking: Choose a favorite pasta recipe. Ask an adult to help you prepare and bring the pasta to class.

4. Math: Using the recipe from Activity #3 above, double the recipe and write the new measurements. Using the original recipe, halve the recipe and write the new measurements.

5. Compare/Contrast: List the similarities and differences between Granny Torrelli's story of Pardo, herself, and Violetta and the situation involving Bailey, Rosie, and Janine.

Pasta
Janine–Sauce

Janine visits Bailey at Rosie's house to ask about her Braille lesson. Granny Torrelli reminds Rosie to be polite and stay calm. Granny Torrelli continues her story about Violetta and Pardo, recalling the time she cut off Violetta's hair. Her plan to make Violetta unattractive failed, however, when Pardo found Violetta even more beautiful with her new "haircut." Bailey asks Rosie if she is jealous of Janine, making Rosie even angrier. Granny Torrelli then tells them that Pardo became jealous when a young man named Marco moved to the village and thought Granny was "very enchanting."

Vocabulary
slink
wretched
heaves
flounder
uttering
kneads
oregano
dribbles
wee
enchanting
flicks

Discussion Questions

1. When Janine asks about Granny Torrelli, Rosie responds with, "This is Granny Torrelli. She's mine" (p. 98). Why does Rosie respond this way? *(Answers will vary but may include that she is afraid Janine will try to monopolize Granny's attention as she has Bailey's.)*

2. Explain how Granny's "one quick look...full of meaning" (p. 101) is both a warning and a comfort to Rosie. *(Granny is warning Rosie not to say or do something to Janine that she will regret but also assuring Rosie that she understands her feelings.)*

3. What is Granny Torrelli's intention when she whispers "Violetta" in Rosie's ear as Janine leaves? *(Answers will vary but may include that Granny Torrelli recognizes the similarities between Rosie's situation with Janine and her own with Violetta.)*

4. What does Granny Torrelli do to Violetta? How does she feel about her actions? Would you have reacted the same way if you were in Granny Torrelli's situation? *(She tells Violetta that she would look nice with shorter hair, and she cuts Violetta's hair. She is shocked and ashamed of what she has done, calling herself "a monster." Answers will vary.)*

5. Why do you think Granny Torrelli leaves Bailey and Rosie alone in the kitchen after completing her story about cutting Violetta's hair? *(Answers will vary but may include that Granny tends to leave the room after making a point that she wants Rosie and Bailey to reflect upon. Granny wants Rosie to realize that the results of jealous actions are often not what we intend.)*

6. Why doesn't Rosie tell Bailey that she is jealous of Janine? *(Answers will vary but may include that Rosie thought Bailey would laugh at her or think she was ridiculous.)*

7. Rosie is very angry at Bailey's response when she asks him whether he could like Janine more than her. How do you think Rosie wanted Bailey to respond? *(Answers will vary but may include that Rosie wanted Bailey to sound more certain and answer "No.")*

8. Analyze Rosie's statement, "I stop being mad at Bailey while my hands are on his" (p. 113). Why do you think touching Bailey allows Rosie to forget her anger? *(Answers will vary but may include that when she touches Bailey, Rosie is able to calm down a bit and remember how much she cares about Bailey. Janine seems like a minor problem when Rosie is near Bailey.)*

9. How is Marco both helpful and a nuisance to Granny Torrelli? *(Marco annoys Granny with his constant presence, but he also makes Pardo jealous, which is satisfying to Granny.)*

10. How is Granny Torrelli's story relevant to Rosie and Bailey? *(Answers will vary but should include that in some ways, Granny and Pardo's situation mirrors that of Rosie and Bailey.)*

Supplementary Activities

1. Literary Elements: Continue adding to your Metaphors and Similes chart.

2. Literary Elements: The author uses many words that appeal to the fives senses as Granny Torrelli prepares the pasta sauce. Using the Senses Chart on page 23 of this guide, list words from the novel that evoke each of the five senses.

3. Drama: Write dialogue to accompany the events Rosie imagines in the first paragraph on page 120 of the novel.

Pasta
The Yellow House–The Pasta Party

Rosie notices a new family moving in down the street, and Bailey becomes jealous and distant when he discovers that the family includes two boys the same age as him and Rosie. Granny Torrelli recalls how Violetta began pursuing Marco when she discovered he was interested in Granny. This angered Granny Torelli, but after caring for a sick baby on the verge of death, she realizes that there are more important things with which to be concerned. Granny's story causes Rosie to think about what is important in her own life, and she decides to invite Janine to the pasta party. The party is a great success, and Rosie discovers that nothing can come between her and Bailey because they are true friends.

Vocabulary
agitated
annoyed
mumbles
assessing
sly
glance
pounce
lullabies
zinnias
awkward

Discussion Questions

1. Why does Rosie think, "Double Marco!" when she sees the family moving in down the street? *(Answers will vary. Suggestion: The family includes two boys about her age. She imagines both boys developing an interest in her and making Bailey jealous.)*

2. How does Bailey feel? How do you know? *(Bailey is angry. He is tossing the meatballs into the pot instead of gently setting them in.)*

3. Do you think Granny Torrelli's "little pause" is a genuine need to excuse herself, or is she leaving for Rosie and Bailey's benefit? Explain your answer. *(Answers will vary.)*

4. Do you think Rosie is justified in purposefully aggravating Bailey? Why or why not? *(Answers will vary.)*

5. Do you think Bailey has the right to be angry? Why or why not? *(Answers will vary.)*

6. What does Bailey mean when he says, "The web is getting very tangled" (p. 131)? *(Answers will vary. Suggestions: The Granny, Pardo, Violetta, and Marco story gets complicated when Violetta shifts her attention to Marco. Also, the Rosie, Bailey, and Janine story could get more complicated with the new neighbor boys moving in.)*

7. Why does Granny Torrelli tell the story of the sick baby? How do you think this story affects Rosie and Bailey? *(Answers will vary but may include that it helps them put things in perspective and realize that there are more important things in life than their small arguments.)*

8. Analyze Rosie's thoughts in the last paragraph on page 137 of the novel. How has Rosie changed? *(Answers will vary but may include that Rosie has matured since listening to Granny Torrelli's stories. She knows she cannot control everything and that she should take comfort in the happiness she has right now.)*

9. What does Rosie mean when she thinks, "my world seems a little bigger" (p. 141)? *(Answers will vary. Suggestions: Rosie has learned to find space in her life to include more friends than just Bailey. She is also aware that there are more important things in life than her minor problems.)*

Supplementary Activities

1. Art: Illustrate a scene from this section of the novel based on the description given by the author.

2. Writing: After completing the novel, add to your life lessons journal.

Post-reading Discussion Questions

1. From whose viewpoint is the story told? How would the story be different had it been told from Bailey's viewpoint? *(Rosie's; Answers will vary.)*

2. Which character in the novel do you most relate to? Why? *(Answers will vary.)*

3. What lessons did you learn from the novel? How can you apply them to your own life? *(Answers will vary.)*

4. How is the title appropriate for the novel? *(Answers will vary. Suggestion: It is the main activity in the novel, during which Rosie and Bailey learn important lessons from Granny Torrelli.)*

5. Discuss how you feel about the lesson Granny learns from the sick baby and the lesson Rosie learns from Granny—that the world is a big place that includes more than just you. *(Answers will vary.)*

6. Do you agree or disagree with Bailey's feelings that he should have special abilities that Rosie does not? Why? *(Answers will vary.)*

7. Is Rosie the type of friend you would like to have? Is Bailey? Why or why not? *(Answers will vary.)*

8. What qualities make Granny Torrelli a good grandmother? Explain your answer. *(Answers will vary.)*

9. What is the most humorous event in the novel? Why do you think so? *(Answers will vary but could include Rosie's attempt to train a guide dog, Violetta's haircut by Granny, Granny comparing heaven to a big pasta party, etc.)*

10. What is the saddest event in the novel? Why so you think so? *(Answers will vary but could include Pardo's death, Granny never taking the opportunity to apologize to Pardo, Bailey's father leaving the family, taking care of the sick baby, etc.)*

11. What purpose do Granny Torrelli's parallel stories serve in the novel? *(Answers will vary but could include that she uses them to show Rosie that others have similar experiences and how they deal with them.)*

12. The author uses flashback to tell about events that have already happened before Granny and Rosie cook in the family kitchen. Do you think this is a good technique to use in this novel? Why or why not? *(Answers will vary.)*

13. Do you think Rosie changes in the novel? Why or why not? *(Answers will vary but could include that she becomes less selfish, more open to the feelings of others, realizes that her world includes more than just herself and Bailey, etc.)*

14. Explain the significance of cooking in the novel. *(Answers will vary.)*

15. Would you change the ending of the novel? If so, what would the new ending be? *(Answers will vary.)*

16. Has this novel changed your views of people who are different from you or who have disabilities? If so, in what ways? *(Answers will vary.)*

Post-reading Extension Activities

Writing

1. Write at least five alternate titles for the novel.

2. Pretend you are Granny Torrelli, and write a letter of apology to Pardo.

3. Pretend you are Pardo, and write a letter to Granny after she arrives in America.

4. Write a letter to Sharon Creech asking what inspired her to write the novel. Ask specific questions about the story that might not have been answered or that you would like to know more about.

5. Write a haiku or an acrostic poem to describe each of the three major characters in the novel—Granny Torrelli, Rosie, and Bailey.

Listening/Speaking

6. Choose an event in the novel, and record an audio diary entry from Bailey's point of view.

Critical Thinking

7. Complete the Character Chart on page 24 of this guide.

Art

8. The author uses vivid action verbs to show what the characters are doing. Choose a chapter from the novel, and draw a comic strip of your favorite scene.

9. Research various types of visual impairment, and create a poster about one type.

10. Create a collage representing Rosie's feelings on her first day of school when Bailey was not there.

Assessment for *Granny Torrelli Makes Soup*

Assessment is an ongoing process. The following ten items can be completed during study of the novel. Once finished, the student and teacher will check the work. Points may be added to indicate the level of understanding.

Name _____ Date _____

Student   **Teacher**

_____   _____   1. Write ten original sentences using words from the vocabulary lists.

_____   _____   2. Write a ten-question quiz and exchange with a partner.

_____   _____   3. Identify five events from the novel that are told in flashback.

_____   _____   4. Complete the Story Map on page 25 of this guide. Be sure to write detailed responses.

_____   _____   5. Write an essay that compares and contrasts Rosie and Bailey, Bailey and Pardo, or Rosie and Granny Torrelli.

_____   _____   6. Complete a Character Web for Rosie, Bailey, and Granny Torrelli using the graphic on page 27 of this guide.

_____   _____   7. Complete the Sequence chart on page 28 of this guide.

_____   _____   8. Rewrite one of the events in the novel from Bailey's point of view.

_____   _____   9. With a partner, role-play a scene from the novel.

_____   _____   10. Complete the Thematic Analysis chart on page 29 of this guide.

Using Predictions

We all make predictions as we read—little guesses about what will happen next, how a conflict will be resolved, which details will be important to the plot, which details will help fill in our sense of a character. Students should be encouraged to predict, to make sensible guesses as they read the novel.

As students work on their predictions, these discussion questions can be used to guide them: What are some of the ways to predict? What is the process of a sophisticated reader's thinking and predicting? What clues does an author give to help us make predictions? Why are some predictions more likely to be accurate than others?

Create a chart for recording predictions. This could either be an individual or class activity. As each subsequent chapter is discussed, students can review and correct their previous predictions about plot and characters as necessary.

Use the facts and ideas the author gives.

Use your own prior knowledge.

Apply any new information (i.e., from class discussion) that may cause you to change your mind.

Predictions

_____

_____

_____

_____

Prediction Chart

What characters have we met so far?	What is the conflict in the story?	What are your predictions?	Why did you make these predictions?

Crossword Puzzle

Directions: Select ten vocabulary words from this guide. Create a crossword puzzle answer key by filling in the grid below. Be sure to number the squares for each word. Blacken any spaces not used by the letters. Then, write clues to the crossword puzzle. Number the clues to match the numbers in the squares. The teacher will give each student a blank grid. Make a blank copy of your crossword puzzle for other students to answer. Exchange your clues with someone else and solve the blank puzzle s/he gives you. Check the completed puzzles with the answer keys.

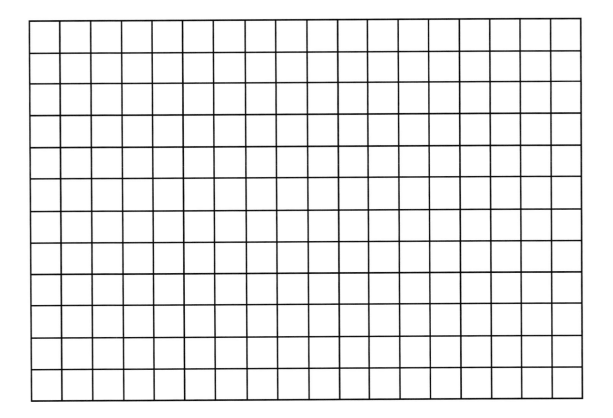

Effects of Reading

Directions: When reading, each part of a book may affect you in a different way. Think about how parts of the novel affected you in different ways. Did some parts make you laugh? cry? want to do something to help someone? Below, list one part of the book that touched each of the following parts of the body: your head (made you think), your heart (made you feel), your funny bone (made you laugh), or your feet (spurred you to action).

Your head	Your heart

Your funny bone	Your feet

Venn Diagram

Directions: Use the Venn diagram below to compare and contrast Granny Torrelli "losing" Nero and Rosie thinking Bailey is lost.

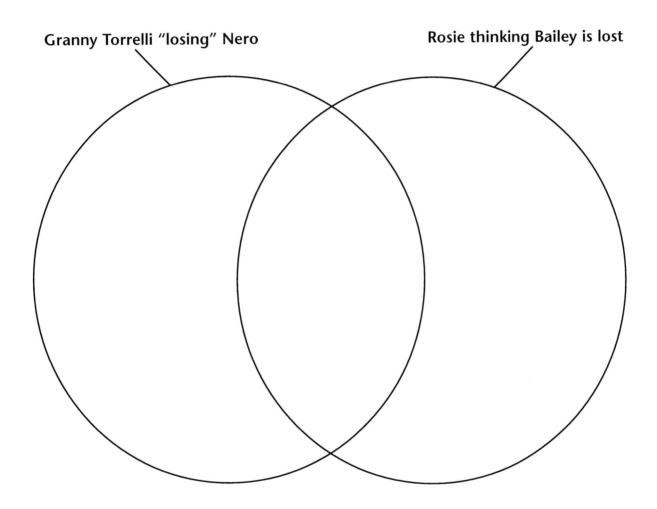

Granny Torrelli "losing" Nero

Rosie thinking Bailey is lost

Metaphors and Similes

A **metaphor** is a comparison between two unlike objects. For example, "he was a human tree." A **simile** is a comparison between two unlike objects that uses the words *like* or *as*. For example, "the color of her eyes was like the cloudless sky."

Directions: Complete the chart below by listing metaphors and similes from the novel, as well as the page numbers on which they are found. Identify metaphors with an "M" and similes with an "S." Translate the comparisons in your own words, and then list the objects being compared.

Metaphors/Similes	Ideas/Objects Being Compared
1. Translation:	
2. Translation:	
3. Translation:	

Senses Chart

Directions: In the chart below, list words from the novel that evoke each of the five senses.

Taste	Touch	Sight	Smell	Sound

Character Chart

Directions: In the boxes across from each of the feelings, describe an incident or time in the book when each of the listed characters experienced that feeling. You may use "not applicable" if you cannot find an example.

	Rosie	Bailey	Granny Torrelli	Pardo
Frustration				
Anger				
Fear				
Humiliation				
Relief				
Triumph				

Story Map

Directions: Choose either Part I or Part II of the novel and complete the story map.

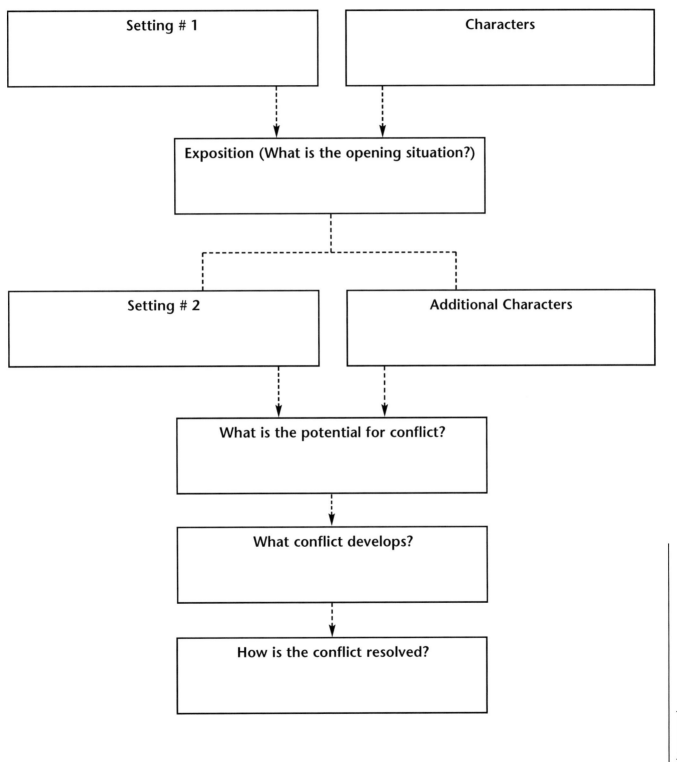

Setting # 1

Characters

Exposition (What is the opening situation?)

Setting # 2

Additional Characters

What is the potential for conflict?

What conflict develops?

How is the conflict resolved?

Using Character Attribute Webs

Character attribute webs are simply a visual representation of a character from the novel. They provide a systematic way for students to organize and recap the information they have about a particular character. Attribute webs may be used after reading the novel to recapitulate information about a particular character, or completed gradually as information unfolds. They may be completed individually or as a group project.

One type of character attribute web uses these divisions:

- How a character acts and feels. (How does the character act? How do you think the character feels? How would you feel if this happened to you?)

- How a character looks. (Close your eyes and picture the character. Describe him/her.)

- Where a character lives. (Where and when does the character live?)

- How others feel about the character. (How does another specific character feel about the character?)

In group discussion about the characters described in student attribute webs, the teacher can ask for backup proof from the novel. Inferential thinking can be included in the discussion.

Character Web

Directions: Complete the chart below. Cite evidence from the story as you fill in information.

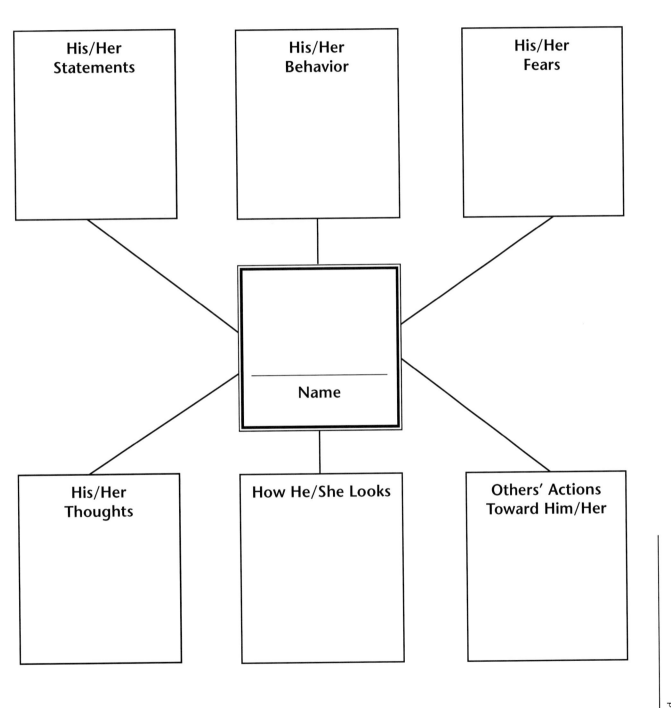

Sequence

Directions: The action of the novel is not told in the proper sequence. After reading the novel, list six events in the order they actually happened.

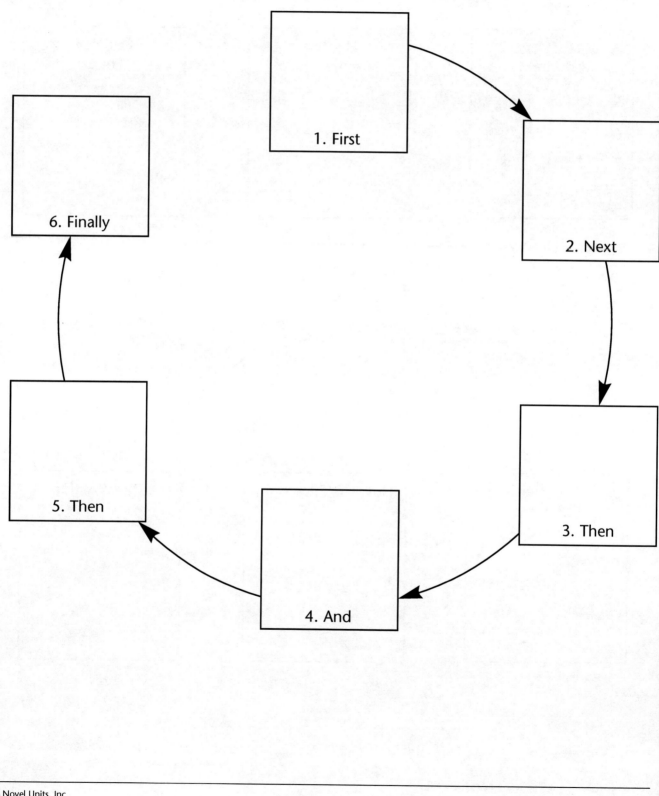

Thematic Analysis

Directions: Choose a theme from the book to be the focus of your word web. Complete the web and then answer the question in each starred box.

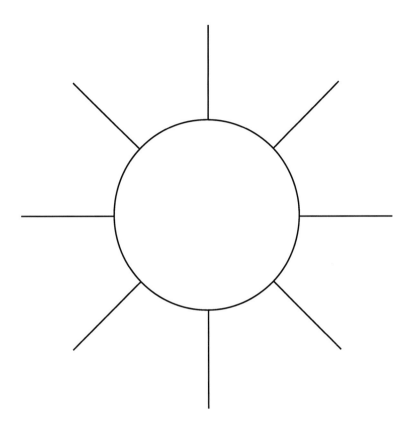

 What is the author's main message?

 What did you learn from the book?

Linking Novel Units® Lessons to National and State Reading Assessments

During the past several years, an increasing number of students have faced some form of state-mandated competency testing in reading. Many states now administer state-developed assessments to measure the skills and knowledge emphasized in their particular reading curriculum. The discussion questions and post-reading questions in this Novel Units® Teacher Guide make excellent open-ended comprehension questions and may be used throughout the daily lessons as practice activities. The rubric below provides important information for evaluating responses to open-ended comprehension questions. Teachers may also use scoring rubrics provided for their own state's competency test.

Please note: The Novel Units® Student Packet contains optional open-ended questions in a format similar to many national and state reading assessments.

Scoring Rubric for Open-Ended Items

3-Exemplary	Thorough, complete ideas/information Clear organization throughout Logical reasoning/conclusions Thorough understanding of reading task Accurate, complete response
2-Sufficient	Many relevant ideas/pieces of information Clear organization throughout most of response Minor problems in logical reasoning/conclusions General understanding of reading task Generally accurate and complete response
1-Partially Sufficient	Minimally relevant ideas/information Obvious gaps in organization Obvious problems in logical reasoning/conclusions Minimal understanding of reading task Inaccuracies/incomplete response
0-Insufficient	Irrelevant ideas/information No coherent organization Major problems in logical reasoning/conclusions Little or no understanding of reading task Generally inaccurate/incomplete response

Notes

Notes